TABLE OF CONTENTS

ACRONYMS

ROK	Republic of Korea
DOS	Department of State
DOD	Department of Defense
USG	United States Government
DSCA	Defense Security Cooperation Agency
UNC	United Nations Command
DPRK	Democratic People's Republic of Korea

TABLES

INTRODUCTION

"Indeed, as we end today's wars, we will focus on a broader range of challenges and opportunities, including the security and prosperity of the Asia Pacific"

– President Barrack Obama

The application of alliances to achieve political ends and prevent, or sometime entice war is a concept which dates back as far as the Peloponnesian War. The very threat of war can create friction and uncertainty between and within enemy and friendly forces, including coalitions. With the growing complexity of a globalized world, the necessity for political, economic, and military alliances and coalitions will be critical for gaining and maintaining stability around the globe. Building partnership capacity with South Korea is a cornerstone to our deterrence efforts in the Pacific region and security assistance and cooperation are integral tools used to gain and maintain stability with North Korea. The study of security assistance and cooperation prior to and following the Korean War will hopefully glean some insight into more effective and efficient ways to use security cooperation as a means to achieve positive military, political, and economic ends and better determine the efficacy of security cooperation on preventing future wars within the context of constrained military budgets.

The United States' insufficient investment in security assistance and cooperation to build the capacity of the Republic of Korea's (ROK) military before the start of the Korean War contributed to the ROK's inability to deter or effectively conduct military operations. Since the Korean War, the U.S. strategy to deter North Korean aggression and maintaining security and stability in the Pacific precipitated the need for increased security assistance and cooperation to the ROK. In an era of globalization, the security of the Korean peninsula continues to evolve in relation to the increasing military capabilities and uncertainty of North Korean strategic objectives. The U.S. investment in security cooperation in Korea following the Korean War enabled the U.S. to gradually withdraw forces from the peninsula while simultaneously building ROK capabilities and deterring a North Korean invasion. Recent history shows that the optimal number of U.S. military presence on the peninsula to achieve deterrence in Korea is 25,000.[2] Research and analysis of the history of U.S. presence in relation to the continued increase in ROK military capacity will provide future insight into what the minimum amount of U.S. presence and ROK capacity is required to deter North Korean aggression.

In order to achieve stability in Korea, U.S. policy states "we will maintain peace on the Korean Peninsula by effectively working with allies and other regional states to deter and defend against provocation from North Korea, which is actively pursuing a nuclear weapons program."[3] The way in which the United States Government (USG) achieves this policy objective is through security assistance programs managed by the Defense Security Cooperation Agency (DSCA). The means to maintain peace and effective deterrence on the Korean Peninsula are through the combination of security assistance programs managed and executed by the Department of State (DOS) and the security cooperation programs managed and executed by the Department of Defense (DOD). This study of U.S.-ROK relations and the Korean War will focus on one particular security assistance program, Foreign Military Sales (FMS), and security cooperation programs to include combined operations and combined exercises. The correlation of how these programs shaped the events leading to the Korean War and the evolution of U.S.-ROK security assistance and cooperation over the course of the last century will illustrate the importance of

---

[2] United States Department of Defense, "Active Duty Military Strength & Other Personnel Statistics," http://www.defense.gov/faq/pis/mil_strength.html (accessed December 11, 2012).

[3] U.S. Department of Defense, *Sustaining U.S. Global Leadership:Priorities for the 21st Century Defense* (Washington, D.C., 2012), 2.

security assistance and cooperation to building partnership capacity in order to prevent future conflict on the Korean Peninsula.

Alliances are the foundation for continued stability and security in Korea and the synergy created by the U.S.-ROK alliance enhances the overall stability within the Pacific region. The U.S. Military acknowledges the strategic importance of alliances as one of five U.S. national security challenges and mandates in Joint Publication 3-0 (*Joint Operations*) that "[e]stablishing, maintaining, and enhancing security cooperation among our alliances and partners is important to strengthen the global security framework of the United States and its partners."[4] Diplomatic, information, and economic instruments of national power play a critical role in attaining this end state, however, the efforts of security assistance and cooperation between the U.S. and ROK will be the most effective demonstration of power projection and ultimately the most effective means for deterrence and peace in the Pacific region.

The political environment and U.S. national strategic objectives from late 19th century to 1950 precluded the U.S. from acknowledging and executing sufficient security assistance and cooperation efforts before the Korean War. Following the Korean War, the bolstered security assistance and cooperation efforts in South Korea created a stable, secure environment, and presents a good model for successful execution of security assistance and cooperation in support of nations of vital U.S. national interest. The gradual degradation of security assistance and cooperation in Korea because of future fiscal restraints requires an analysis on the level and nature of future engagement required in relation to what the U.S. can afford both fiscally and politically. This is critical for determining the most efficient security assistance and cooperation requirements to retain effective deterrence against future hostile actions on the Korean peninsula.

---

[4] Joint Staff, *Joint Publication 3-0: Joint Operations* (Washington, D.C., 2011), x.

An analysis of this correlation will potentially help future researchers and analysts identify the critical point where the minimum amount of U.S. security cooperation efforts will continue to maintain successful deterrence against an invasion from North Korea.

METHODOLOGY

A combination of quantitative and qualitative methods of analysis will assess the effectiveness of security cooperation efforts to deter hostile aggression in South Korea. The research and analysis of quantitative data through primary sources will focus on the number and type of forces allocated to security cooperation, a qualitative assessment on the deterrence effects of military exercises conducted, and the economic investment through foreign military sales and other security cooperation efforts as a percentage of military spending. The research and analysis of qualitative data through secondary sources will focus on a comparison of current and past U.S. policy in South Korea, a comparison of past and present doctrine and practices for security cooperation, and an assessment on the effectiveness of the Korean Military Advisory Group.

The analysis of the quantitative and qualitative data of security cooperation will illustrate the correlation of the effectiveness of deterrence in relation to the amount of security cooperation efforts. Three time periods will be examined in this monograph to conduct this analysis, 1882-1905, 1945-1950, and 1950-2013. Additionally, this monograph will provide a qualitative assessment on the impact of nuclear and ballistic missile capabilities of North Korea on security cooperation and its impact on the efficacy of security cooperation and future deterrence. The expected-utility model of deterrence presented by Paul Huth and Bruce Russett will be used to assess the effectiveness of U.S. security cooperation activities to deter a North Korean invasion.

The expected-utility model of deterrence hypothesizes that a deterrent threat is effective to the extent it can produce cost-benefit calculations on the part of the potential attacker in which the expected utility of an attack would be less than the expected utility of forgoing the attack. This deterrence model makes three critical assumptions. First, it involves analysis of inference about the utilities decision makers attach to outcomes, and the probabilities they attach to achievement of those outcomes. Second, the key decision (to attack or not, to respond to the attack with force or not) is made by single decision-makers or by small groups operating as units.

5

Lastly, the decision-makers are rational expected-utility maximizers.[5] Given these assumptions, the expected-utility model suggests that the potential attacker will calculate the cost-benefit to attack or not to attack a defender. This cost-benefit calculation includes two major factors. First, the attacker will assess if it has sufficient military capability to defeat the defender.[6] Second, the attacker will assess the motivation, commitment, and resolve of the allies of the defender. Consideration of the combination of these two factors will determine the calculus for an attacker to make the decision to attack or not to attack. The two benchmarks used to determine the effectiveness of deterrence to analyze the research in this monograph will be local military strength in some combination of both U.S. and ROK forces and the strength of the ties of mutual interest between the U.S. and ROK by examining U.S. policy.[7]

---

[5] Paul Huth and Bruce Russett, "What Makes Deterrence Work? Cases from 1900 to 1980," *World Politics* 36, no. 4 (July 1984): 498-500.

[6] Ibid., 501.

[7] Ibid., 524.

SECURITY COOPERATION IN KOREA 1882 TO 1905

One of the first American attempts at government sponsored military assistance and

cooperation to a foreign country began in Korea in the 19th century. During this period, a number

of attempts were made by several Western powers to open an isolationist Korea to trade.[8] These

cursory efforts to establish a trade relationship with Korea could not predict the burgeoning of

this "Hermit Kingdom" would later constitute a vital security interest to American military and

economic strategy.[9] During the reign of King Kojong from 1863-1907, he transformed an isolated

and anti-foreign country to an open one struggling for autonomy and political identity in a

political environment dominated by Western and Asian imperialism.[10] Before the Korean-

Japanese Treaty of 1876 and the Korean-American Treaty of 1882, Korea was politically

dependent on China as a traditional suzerain. The rising political tension between Korea and

China before the Sino-Japanese War from 1894-1895 was due to Korea's desire to decrease its

dependency on China while China continued to try to control Korea in the name of suzerain-

dependency relations.[11]

During this time of increased tensions between Korea, Japan, and China, the U.S.

attempted to open sea lines of communications with Korea. As far back as 1871, the U.S. Navy

made landings in Korea, first on a military expedition and later to seek treaties for American

trade.[12] The U.S. military during that time represented "the forward edge of American foreign

---

[8] Richard P. Weinert, "The Original KMAG," *Military Review* XLV, no. 6 (June 1965):
93.

[9] Yur-Bok Lee and Wayne Patterson, *Korean-American Relations 1866-1997* (Albany:
State University of New York Press), 1.

[10] Ibid., 11.

[11] Ibid., 15.

[12] James P. Finley, *The US Military Experience in Korea 1871-1982: In the Vanguard of*

policy and the sole executor of those policies."[13] The close nature of Korean-American relations today has an early history of violent conflict. In 1866, a U.S. merchantman, the *General Sherman*, was sunk in the Taedong River and subsequently all hands on the ship were massacred by Koreans determined to resist foreign "contamination."[14] Five years following the *General Sherman* massacre, the U.S. Minister to China, Frederick F. Low, journeyed to Korea under the protection of Rear Admiral John Rodgers, commanding the Asiatic squadron.[15] Attempts to negotiate a commercial treaty with Korea resulted in a battle between the Korean guards on Kanghwa Island and Admiral Rodgers' squadron, resulting in 350 Korean dead and three Americans killed.[16]

The isolationist policy of Korea in the late 19th century created a deteriorating security situation in Korea and in great need of military reform. Although Korea possessed proud military traditions, clan rivalry, factionalism, and corruption severely degraded the efficacy of the military institutions.[17] In recognition of Korea's vulnerabilities in its inability to secure itself, Kojong became interested in military reform and began sending Korean students to train in both Japan and China.[18]

ROK-US Relations (San Francisco: Command Historian's Office, Secretary Joint Staff, Hqs, USFK/EUSA), 1.

[13] Ibid.

[14] Ibid.

[15] Ibid.

[16] Ibid., 2.

[17] Donald M. Bishop, "Shared Failure: American Military Advisors in Korea, 1888-1896" (Transactions of the Royal Asiatic Society, Korea Branch 58 (1983)), 53.

[18] Ibid., 54

Despite the monarch's efforts, the instability, corruption, and insecurity of Korea's military manifested itself in the form of violent protest in July of 1882 and resulted in the attack of government offices, the palace, Japanese Legation, and barracks.[19] Kojong was deposed for thirty-three days during this revolt until China removed the ex-regent and restored the king.[20] The Soldiers' revolt of 1882 set the foundation for Kojong's lack of confidence and trust in his military and laid the foundation for his desire to look beyond the regional powers of China and Japan for military assistance.

Following these volatile beginnings to Korean-American relations, the U.S. government's motivation to open negotiations of a treaty of commerce coupled with an emerging Korean desire for modernization helped improve this relationship towards the end of the 19th century. The Koreans realized during this time that the U.S. was the least likely Western nation to try to take over Korea because of the great geographic distance from Korea and its apparent commercial and moral interests in Korea.[21] For this reason, in 1882, the U.S. government became the first Western power to conclude a treaty with Korea and the Koreans began to request American technical assistance in modernizing the country.[22]

The genesis of the Korean perception of the U.S. as the "Elder Brother" began with this treaty and the presence of the U.S. military, albeit limited presence, further increased the Korean expectation of the U.S. to help Korea secure their independence. In contrast to the Korean understanding of the Treaty, the U.S. government's primary strategic interests did not include the security of Korea but was more concerned with the protection of American seamen and the

---

[19] Bishop, "Shared Failure," 54.

[20] Ibid.

[21] Lee and Patterson, *Korean-American Relations 1866-1997*, 13.

[22] Weinert, "The Original KMAG," 94-95.

9

opening of trade.[23] Because the U.S. government found little reason to create a more secure alliance, leverage nonmilitary advantages, read intentions, build trust, convert opinions, and manage perceptions with Korea during this time – all tasks that demand an exceptional ability to understand people, their culture, and their motivation, the lack of political support sowed the seeds of future war.[24]

Despite the initial attempts to forge an economic, military, and political alliance with Korea, as far as the U.S. Department of State was concerned, beyond obligating itself to deal with Korea as an independent nation, it never felt committed to ensure and guarantee the integrity and independence of Korea.[25] This official U.S. policy on Korea starkly contrasted with how the Koreans interpreted the Korean-American Treaty. King Kojong wanted the United States not only to lead the modernization of Korea but more importantly to ensure or guarantee the independent status of Korea as a kind of new elder brother.[26] This diametrically opposed understanding of the treaty would ultimately lead the U.S. government to recognize Japan as a protectorate of Korea following the Russo-Japanese War, sever all foreign policy relations and shut down the Korean legation in Seoul and Washington by 28 November 1905.[27]

The tumultuous Korean-American relations in the late 19th and early 20th centuries illuminates the immaturity of the political and diplomatic dynamic between a growing Western super power and a third world nation desperately trying to establish independence. The Third

---

[23] Lee and Patterson, *Korean-American Relations 1866-1997*, 17.

[24] Freedman, Lawrence, *Transformation of Strategic Affairs* (New York: Routledge for the International Institute for Strategic Studies), 22.

[25] Lee and Patterson, *Korean-American Relations 1866-1997*, 15.

[26] Ibid, 16.

[27] Finley, *The US Military Experience 1871-1982*, 42.

World Security School hypothesizes that in order for a third world country, such as Korea during the late 19th and early 20th century, to overcome their own insecurities it would be necessary to create a strong security sector under strong leadership.[28] Korea during this time was a weak and poor state because of its relative weakness in comparison to Japan and China, its lack of autonomy, its ineffective military, and the vulnerability and lack of room for maneuver, both economically and politically. The continuing internal and external instability within Korea and the East Asian region were inextricably linked to Korea's inability to become a dominant and independent state in the Pacific. Because the U.S. government's primary interest with Korea was trade and not nation building, the growth of the independence of Korea had little to no influence on U.S. security interests.

As Japan's economic, military, and political dominance in the region grew in the early 20th century U.S. interest in maintaining diplomatic and economic interests with Korea began to wane. The Japanese victory of the Sino-Japanese War (1894-1895) resolved the rivalry between Japan and China for predominance over Korea and concluded with the Treaty of Shimonoseki, with China recognizing Korean independence.[29] America's policy of maintaining neutrality during the deteriorating political situation on the peninsula led to the failure of the military mission.[30] As early as 1900, President Roosevelt dictated this policy of neutrality with Korea and ultimately concluded that Japan should control Korea as a check upon Russian expansion.[31] Despite the minimal political and security interest in Korea, the U.S. government during the

---

[28] Steve Smith, "The Increasing Insecurity of Security Studies: Conceptualizing Security in the Last Twenty Years" *Contemporary Security Policy* 20:3 (September 2007): 81.

[29] R. Ernest Dupuy and Trevor Dupuy, *The Encyclopedia of Military History from 3500 B.C. to the Present* (New York: Harper & Row Publishers, 1986), 866.

[30] Weinert, "The Original KMAG," 99.

[31] Lee and Patterson, *Korean-American Relations 1866-1997*, 19.

period from 1882 to 1905 planted the seeds for security assistance by establishing and deploying the first military advisory group to Korea in 1888 at the repeated requests of King Kojong.

The First Military Advisory Group

Against a tumultuous Western and Asian imperialist political backdrop and in the interest of modernizing the Korean military forces, in 1883 Kojong requested the services of American officers to train a nucleus of forty cadets and offered the second highest military rank in the Kingdom to the senior officer in the delegation.[32] This request precipitated the beginning of the first advisory mission to Korea, which would be realized in 1888 with the deployment of Brigadier General William McEntire Dye to serve as His Majesty's Chief of Military Instructor on 7 April 1888.[33] Assisted by Colonel E.H. Cummins, Major John G. Lee, and Captain F.J. Nienstead, this advisory team attempted to lay the foundation for a modern Korean military.[34] It is important to note that this military mission to Korea was not an official US undertaking, but it did have the full support and *de facto* sponsorship of the State Department.[35] Constitutional and bureaucratic impediments coupled with lukewarm attitudes of American officials delayed the deployment of the advisors by five years.[36]

In conjunction with Kojong's request for military advisors to modernize the military systems and training, he requested the procurement of new American weapon systems in an effort to modernize his military's antiquated equipment. In 1883, the Korean Government purchased

---

[32] Finley, *The US Military Experience 1871-1982*, 5.

[33] Ibid.

[34] Ibid.

[35] Weinert, "The Original KMAG," 99.

[36] Lee and Patterson, *Korean-American Relations 1866-1997*, 22.

4,000 Remington breech-loading rifles from the United States.[37] With the impetus of military reform and the improving diplomatic relations, Kojong requested and acquired six Gatling guns, ammunition reloading equipment, and the descriptions and plans of American torpedoes (mines) over the course of the next three years following the acquisition of the rifles.[38] The sale of these weapons represents the first foreign military sales to Korea.

The Commanding General of the Army, Philip Sheridan, recommended Dye as chief of the Korean military mission. Dye was a West Point graduate, served with distinction on the Western frontier, and had been promoted to brigadier general of volunteers during the Civil War.[39] Cummins was the next most experienced military advisor retiring as a Major in the Confederate Army and later a patrol officer in the District of Columbia and in 1888 he was already sixty-five years old.[40] Dye's second assistant, Dr. John Lee, was a physician with no military experience.[41] His third assistant was Ferdinand Nienstead who was vice-consul and translator in the American consulate at Kobe with only one term of military service as a Navy pay clerk.[42] The first physical presence of security assistance to Korea originated from this inexperienced group of military advisors. They were ill resourced, plagued with internal strife, and as a result, the early efforts of the first military advisory group to Korea proved to be lackluster and ephemeral.

---

[37] Weinert, The Original KMAG, 95.

[38] Ibid., 95-97.

[39] Lee and Patterson, *Korean-American Relations 1866-1997*, 23.

[40] Ibid.

[41] Ibid.

[42] Ibid.

Dye's first mission was to initiate military reform by establishing a military academy, the *Yonmu Kongwon*, in order to train forty military cadets in a modern military tactics.[43] In addition to this task, Kojong directed the training of 160 army noncommissioned officers of his palace guard.[44] In addition to the overwhelming tasks for such a small advisory contingent to conduct the training, the advisors "lacked language ability, specific military skills adapted to Korean needs, and the proper temperaments to work in Korea."[45] A multitude of administrative and personal issues between the members of the KMAG and the Korean government eventually lead to the dismissal of Cummins and Lee in 1889, only a year after their arrival in Korea.[46] Dye and Nienstead continued the KMAG mission even as the number of academy cadets gradually decreased and never received more authority, troops or control than they had at the turn of the decade.[47] After Dye's military contract expired in 1896, the Russian and French military missions aggressively assumed the task of instructing the Korean military with similar results.[48] Dye remained in Korea until 1899 as an unofficial manager of the government farm and the use of U.S. military advisors or any security cooperation activities with Korea ended with his departure until the end of WWII in 1945.

Suffice it to say that the Dye's attempts to modernize the Korean military did not reverse the trend of domestic disorder, the destructive effects of a coups, or violent factional struggles within and from external threats at the turn of the 20th century. The efforts of Dye and his un-

---

[43] Bishop, "Shared Failure," 62.

[44] Ibid.

[45] Ibid., 70.

[46] Lee and Patterson, *Korean-American Relations 1866-1997*, 24.

[47] Bishop, "Shared Failure," 66.

[48] Ibid., 69.

14

experienced, under resourced, and under staffed advisory team were partly to blame for the failure of the first security assistance and cooperation mission to Korea. However, the lack of national commitment of the Korean government and military to implement military reform and lack of educated and experienced Korean leadership to guide the reform made the security cooperation efforts destined for failure. [49] Additionally, the lack of U.S. government support and a strict U.S. policy of positive neutrality with Korea demonstrated the lack of will to fully support the reformation and modernization of the Korean military.

Five decades later, the legacy of Dye's advisory mission would evolve into one of the most heavily studied of the U.S. missions during the 1940s.[50] A change in national military strategy emphasizing military advisory and assistance missions became a tool for exporting the ideological task of combating communist expansion.[51] Despite the efforts of General Dye's advisory mission, the U.S. policy of positive neutrality with Korea's security assistance and cooperation efforts in the late 19th century did not necessitate a significant investment into the security of a third world country torn by competing powers of Japan and China. The failure to modernize and reform the Korean military resulted in an ineffective and sparse Korean local force incapable of preventing its annexation to the Japanese Empire in 1910. According to the expected-utility model of deterrence, the lack of local Korean military strength and limited ties of mutual interests with the U.S. set the conditions for Korea's inability to exercise influence in the region and deter Japanese Imperial rule from 1910 – 1945.[52] President Roosevelt's policy of

---

[49] Bishop, "Shared Failure," 69.

[50] Kendall D. Gott and Michael G. Brooks, *Security Assistance; U.S. and International Historical Perspectives* (Fort Leavenworth: Combat Studies Institute Press, 2006), 36.

[51] Ibid.

[52] Huth and Russett, "What Makes Deterrence Work?" 524.

neutrality precluded the U.S. from investing in Korea's security and establishing the "Elder Brother" alliance King Kojung desired. However, the drastic change in world events fifty years following Dye's initial attempts to export U.S. foreign policy through security assistance and cooperation forced the U.S. as a burgeoning world power to invest politically, economically, and militarily in the security of Korea.

SECURITY COOPERATION IN KOREA 1945 TO 1950

Towards the end of World War II U.S., China, and Great Britain agreed at the 1943 allied conference in Cairo that Korea, which had been under Japanese domination for 40 years, would become a free and independent nation.[53] On 9 September 1945, the Japanese forces formally surrendered to LTG John R. Hodge, Commander of U.S. Army Forces in Korea and XXIV Corps, and established a U.S. Military Government in Korea south of the 38th parallel with three divisions at a strength of 77,600.[54] With the Soviets responsible for and in control of the northern half of Korea north of the 38th parallel, Korea rapidly became fertile ground for tension between the U.S. and Soviet Russia. Korea remained divided into an agricultural south and an industrial north, with disastrous consequences for both economies.[55]

Over the course of the five years between the end of WWII and the beginning of the Korean War, U.S. foreign and security policy in regards to Korea vacillated in the face of a growing Soviet Communist influence in the region. The economic and politically focused U.S. policy during this time invested relatively less on the security assistance and cooperation in support of the South Korean military than the Soviets invested in the North Korean military. In 1945, the policy goal of the U.S. focused on extinguishing the Japanese empire from the peninsula as quickly and bloodlessly as possible and to create a new Japan on the Home Islands.[56] Similarly, the USSR's policy goals were provincial in scope in 1945 as well. The Soviet's aim was to strip northern Korea of any people and property that would help the Soviet Union's

---

[53] Finley, *The US Military Experience 1871-1982*, 42.

[54] Ibid., 43-44.

[55] Ibid., 6.

[56] Alan R. Millett, *The War for Korea, 1950-1951 They Came from the North* (Lawrence: University Press of Kansas, 2010), 11.

postwar recovery.[57] It was not until the end of 1945 that the Soviet policy began shifting to create a Communist buffer state and to mount a campaign to unify all of Korea as soon as the Americans departed south of the 38th parallel.[58]

In addition to the mounting tension between the U.S. and the USSR in regards to the future of a new and independent Korea, the U.S. Army Military Government in Korea was left to fill the gap in the Korean government left by the departure of the Japanese, who occupied virtually every position both in the government and in industry.[59] Initially, the security assistance and cooperation efforts of General Hodge focused on nation building and internal security, not on developing the Korean military for long-term national and independent security. From 1945 to 1948 the maintenance of Korean internal security was the responsibility of the National Police Force (NPF) and the U.S. military organized a Korean Constabulary to assist the NPF and provided police reserves.[60] The agreement for support to South Korea was focused more on economic development than security reflected by the U.S. pledge to "financial, material, and technical assistance to avert economic crisis, promote national recovery, and insure domestic tranquility."[61] Almost all U.S. policy initiatives through 1950 were economic and political; little attention had been given to the U.S. or anyone else's military capabilities.[62] Despite the political neutrality towards supporting significant security assistance to Korea in the first three years after

---

[57] Millett, *The War for Korea*, 11.

[58] Ibid.

[59] Finley, *The US Military Experience 1871-1982*, 4.

[60] Alfred H. Hausrath, *The KMAG Advisor: Role and Problems of the Military Advisor in Developing an Indigenous Army for Combat Operations in Korea* (Chevy Chase: The Johns Hopkins University Operations Research Office, 1957), 8.

[61] Ibid., 8.

[62] John Lewis Gaddis and Paul Nitze, "NSC 68 and the Soviet Threat Reconsidered," *International Security* 4, no. 4 (1980): 171.

their independence, the U.S. military continued to conduct limited security assistance and cooperation activities to improve the internal security through the Korean Constabulary while the senior military leadership in the theater continued to put pressure on the government to provide more.

Despite the tension between the U.S. and Soviet presence on the peninsula, on August 2, 1946, the Supreme Commander for the Allied Powers, General MacArthur, formally requested additional U.S. advisory support for the Korean Coast Guard to President Truman. Specifically, MacArthur requested a detail of 17 officers and 14 enlisted personnel of the U.S. Navy or the U.S. Coast Guard to supervise and train the newly established Korean Coast Guard.[63] In addition to the personnel, he requested the loan of U.S. Naval ships and crafts from U.S. surpluses.[64] The establishment of the Korean Coast Guard was not intended to be the nucleus of a Korean Navy and in order to avoid any semblance of a U.S. sponsored Korean Navy MacArthur insisted that the training of this Korean Coast Guard be carried out by U.S. Coast Guard personnel rather than by U.S. Navy personnel.[65] The sensitivity towards the Soviet Government perception of U.S. security assistance and cooperation activities at this time highlights the growing uncertainty and tension between the U.S. and the USSR. This effort to build the capacity of the Korean naval capacity demonstrated the growing need for security cooperation and assistance required to bolster a credible Korean military.

By 1947, the political tensions between the U.S. and Soviets and their respective developing North Korean and South Korean governments continued to escalate and the feasibility

---

[63] Memorandum for the President, *Training of Korean Coast Guard by United States Coast Guard Personnel* (National Archives: Harry S. Truman Library, 2 August 1946), 1-2.

[64] Ibid., 2.

[65] Ibid.

of a unified Korean government became increasingly untenable. So much that on January 3, 1947 General Hodge issued warnings of an impending invasion of the U.S. zone by Soviet-trained Koreans, and accordingly requested that the US forces be brought up to Table of Organization (T/O) strength.[66] Hodge predicted that the invasion would probably take the form of mass infiltration, rather than of a regular military expedition and that the Soviet army in North Korea, estimated at approximately 150,000 men, would presumably cross the border, unless US troops should withdraw entirely from the peninsula.[67] The growing security threat precipitated a response from the Department of State, with the concurrence of the War Department, and "proposed legislation to authorize appropriations to the President of not to exceed $78,000,000 in fiscal year 1948 for assistance to Korea beyond that assistance provided in the War Department estimates for 1948 now before Congress and involving $137,000,000."[68] The willingness of the U.S. government to almost double the financial investment in the security of Korea marked a limited, yet growing concern for the peninsula and the ideological and political implications to the security interests of the United States.

By the end of 1947, the Central Intelligence Agency reported to President Truman that "Since no effective counterforce can be established by the U.S. in South Korea without the investment of considerable effort over an extended period, U.S. withdrawal would have the effect of leaving South Korea incapable of offering any serious resistance to eventual domination by the North."[69] In spite of the viable security threats to South Korea, President Truman continued a

---

[66] Central Intelligence Group, *The Situation in Korea* (National Archives: Harry S. Truman Library, 3 January 1947), 9.

[67] Ibid.

[68] Memorandum for the President, *Clearance of Proposed Legislation for Aid to Korea* (National Archives: Harry S. Truman Library, 3 June 1947), 1.

[69] Central Intelligence Agency, *Implementation of Soviet Objectives in Korea* (National

narrative primarily supporting the economic and political stability of South Korea with little

emphasis in regards to the investing heavily in their military or a continued U.S. presence on the

peninsula. In June of 1947, President Truman submitted the following message to Congress

outlining his focus for foreign policy in South Korea:

> "A weak Korea, unable to support itself and to sustain its independence, would constantly
> invite trouble. An economically sound and politically stable and united Korea will be an
> active force toward the peace and well-being of all Asia. This objective is of paramount
> importance to the peace and security of the United States. The people of Korea, long
> oppressed, look to America for help and guidance to achieve their freedom and their
> independence. If we are mindful of our interest and are faithful to our ideals, we will not
> fail them." [70]

The major-powers negotiations and UN action continued to fail from 1947-1949 and the

U.S. Government resolved to withdraw from Korea, but promised to continue support to South

Korea within practicable and feasible limits as a means to minimize the adverse effects of

withdrawal. [71] In addition to the existential diplomatic and security issues with the USSR, China,

and North Korea, the internal efforts of the U.S. to establish a democratic and sovereign

government in Korea lacked significant progress handicapped by the political immaturity of the

Korean people. [72] Korean political factions in the south polarized into extremes and pursued their

ends through use of violence, thereby adding to the political instability in Korea. [73]

Archives: Harry S. Truman Library, 18 November 1947), 1.

[70] For Transmission by the President (Harry Truman), *Draft Message on Korea*, (National Archives: Harry S. Truman Library, 3 June 1947), 7.

[71] Kenneth W. Condit, *History of the Joint Chiefs of Staff: The Joint Chiefs of Staff and National Policy Volume II 1947-1949*, (Washington D.C.: Office of Joint History, 1996), 274-275.

[72] National Security Council (NSC), *A Report to the President: The Position of the United States with Respect to Korea*, (National Archives: Harry S. Truman Library, 2 April 1948), 5-6.

[73] NSC, *A Report to the President: The Position of the United States with Respect to Korea*, 5-6.

In conjunction with the internal and external political resistance for continued U.S. presence and support to Korea, a critical factor for withdrawing from the peninsula was the opinion of the Joint Chiefs of Staff who openly stated:

> "the United States had little interest in maintaining its present troops and bases in Korea, where they would be a liability in the event of war. In this eventuality, they could not be maintained there without substantial reinforcement. Moreover, any US offensive operations on the Asian mainland would probably bypass Korea. The occupation force of approximately 45,000 men in Korea could better be used to remedy military manpower shortages in areas of greater strategic significance."[74]

The decision for a complete withdrawal of U.S. forces, however, came at a considerable amount of calculated risk. The U.S. government recognized that the potential extension of Soviet control over all of Korea would enhance the political and strategic position of the Soviet Union with respect to China and Japan and adversely affect the position of the U.S. in the Far East.[75] Additionally, President Truman understood that U.S. friends and allies could interpret withdrawal as a betrayal by the U.S. and incur significant risk by fundamentally re-aligning its friends and allies in the Far East in favor of the Soviet Union.[76] Despite these concerns and risks to national security, the National Security Council ultimately recommended three non-committal approaches on the most prudent action for the U.S. to deal with Korea for President Truman to decide upon.

Ultimately, in 1948 the National Security Council proposed to President Truman three courses of action on how to end the political stalemate with the Soviets. The first option suggested a complete abandonment of the established government.[77] The second option guaranteed the sovereignty of Korea by force of arms if necessary, against external aggression or

---

[74] Condit, *History of the Joint Chiefs of Staff*, 275.

[75] Ibid.

[76] Ibid.

[77] NSC, *A Report to the President: The Position of the United Sates with Respect to Korea*, 8-11.

internal subversion. The last option presented an amalgam of the first two options by establishing

practicable, feasible, and limited conditions of support, as a means of liquidating U.S.

commitment of men and equipment from Korea with the minimum of bad effects. [78] The official

recommendation from the NSC to President Truman stated as follows: "It should be the effort of

the U.S. government through all proper means to effect a settlement of the Korean problem which

would enable the U.S. to withdraw from Korea as soon as possible with the minimum of bad

effects."[79] Because of the competing demands between the internal pressure to withdraw from the

peninsula and the international pressure for the U.S. government to support the development and

security of South Korea, the U.S. government committed continued support through limited

military and economic aid as a means to implement this end.

President Truman and the NSC attempted to mitigate the risk of the withdrawal of

combat forces from the peninsula through the implementation of seven stipulated conditions to

the withdrawal. The most significant proposals by the NSC which Truman agreed to was the U.S.

commitment to the expansion, training, and equipping of the Korean constabulary and the

continuation of military aid through a tailored military advisory group. These proposals served as

a means of providing effective protection for the security of South Korea against any overt act of

aggression by North Korean or other forces.[80] Additionally, a provision was written into the NSC

proposal that the U.S. should encourage continued UN interest and participation in the Korean

problem and should continue to cooperate with the UN.[81] The effort on the U.S. government to

---

[78] NSC, *A Report to the President: The Position of the United Sates with Respect to Korea*, 8-11.

[79] Ibid.

[80] NSC, *A Report to the President: The Position of the United Sates with Respect to Korea*, 11-12.

[81] Ibid., 12.

put pressure on the UN to play a more significant role in the solution to the Korean problem further legitimated the withdrawal of U.S. forces and eventually set the conditions for the approval of the UN resolution to support the war in Korea.

The policy of limited support for South Korea extended to the provision of a degree of assistance for a modest military force and equipment for this force came originally from US surplus stocks but later was provided by grant aid provided under Title III of the Mutual Defense Assistance Act of 1949.[82] The U.S. Army Military Government relinquished governmental control over to the Koreans following the election of its first president, Syngman Rhee, on 15 August 1948 and officially established the Republic of Korea (ROK) as well as the Republic of Korea Army (ROKA) south of the 38th parallel.

Concurrent to the establishment of the ROK, the U.S. State Department established the Provisional Military Advisory Group (PMAG) to assist the ROK in building up its internal security forces, with special emphasis on the National Police Force (NPF).[83] From October 1948 to July 1949 the PMAG assisted the infant republic in the organization, administration, training and equipping of it security forces.[84] The first bilateral agreement between the U.S. and ROK government committed the U.S. to provide sufficient equipment for security forces numbering 104,000, divided between 65,000 ROKA and the remainder 39,000 to security forces made up of police and coast guard, the function of which would be to maintain internal security.[85] This equipment and training represented the most significant security assistance effort to the ROK up until this time. The presence of the U.S. military in South Korea deterred an imminent invasion

---

[82] Condit, *History of the Joint Chiefs of Staff*, 275.

[83] Hausrath, *The KMAG Advisor*, 1.

[84] Ibid., 8.

[85] Hausrath, *The KMAG Advisor*, 8.

from North Korea up until May of 1949 when President Truman approved the final withdrawal of the remaining U.S. troops from Korea.[86]

On 1 July 1949, the Korean Military Advisory Group (KMAG) to Korea was formed and became the only remaining U.S. security assistance force in Korea with an authorized strength of 500 officers and men under the supervision of the State Department and under control of the U.S. Ambassador and became an integral part of the American Mission in Korea (AMIK).[87] The primary mission of the KMAG was "to advise the government of the Republic of Korea in the continued development of the Security Forces of that government."[88] The security cooperation efforts of the KMAG advisors helped the ROKA expand its original four divisions to a total of eight, with a strength of approximately 95,000 men by 25 June 1950, the date of the North Korean invasion of South Korea.[89] Despite the significant effort and progress made by the KMAG advisors, President Truman's policy decision to withdraw U.S. forces from the peninsula created a significant imbalance of local military power between the North Korean Army and the ROKA. According to the expected-utility model of deterrence, the military power gap as a result of President Truman's limited interest in the security of the ROK set the conditions for the North Korean invasion less than 12 months from the withdrawal of U.S. military combat troops. President Truman's limited economic and military policy towards the ROK during this time reflected a relative increase in mutual interest with the ROK as compared to President Roosevelt's policy of neutrality. However, the limited increase in the ties of mutual interest

---

[86] Finley, *The U.S. Military Experience*, 53.

[87] Ibid.

[88] Ibid.

[89] Hausrath, *The KMAG Advisor*, 8-9.

25

between the U.S. and the ROK did not pose a credible immediate deterrent for the impending

invasion from North Korea.

On 25 June 1950, North Korean soldiers crossed the 38th parallel and invaded the ROK with approximately 136,000 ground forces against the 65,000 ROKA ground forces.[90] The actions of the United Nations Security Council provided the international legitimacy to establish a U.S. led coalition to repel the North Korean attack. Specifically, on July 7, 1950, the U.N. Security Council passed Resolution 84 which stated the following:

> "…Recommends that all members providing military forces and assistance pursuant to the aforesaid Security Council Resolutions make such forces and other assistance available to a unified command under the United States…Requests the United States to designate the commander of such forces [and] authorizes the unified command at its discretion to use the United Nations flag in the course of operations against North Korean forces concurrently with the flags of various nations participating."[91]

Soon after the decimation of the ROKA ground forces, the UN Security Council authorized military assistance to the ROK and President Truman placed General MacArthur in command of the UN forces in the theater. With the imminent need to generate and reconstitute ROKA forces in the theater, the KMAG's role became exponentially important to support the war effort.[92] Upon establishment of the UN Command (UNC), the KMAG functioned under the control of U.S. Eighth Army and began to function as a unit, later equivalent to a corps.[93] The actual strength of the KMAG increased from 500 to 3000 in order to assist in reconstituting the decimated ROKA divisions into approximately 591,000 ROKA ground troops by the end of the war.[94]

---

[90] Finley, *The U.S. Military Experience in Korea*, 56.

[91] Donald Boose, Balbina Hwang, Patrick Morgan, Andrew Scobell, *Recalibrating the U.S.-Republic of Korea Alliance* (Carlisle: Strategic Studies Institute, 2003), 71.

[92] Hausrath, *The KMAG Advisor*, 9.

[93] Finley, 9.

[94] Ibid., 102.

In spite of the withdrawal of U.S. forces and the subsequent North Korean invasion the following year, President Truman and the NSC's decided to retain the KMAG capability in Korea prior to the start of the Korean War. This security cooperation initiative increased the capability and capacity of the U.S. Eighth Army to quickly increase the strength of its advising capability from 500 to 3,000 in order to quickly rebuild, train, and equip an effective ROKA.[95] The limited, but crucial investment of military expertise leading to a rapid build up of ROKA capabilities demonstrates the significant return on investment in security assistance programs prior to the start of the Korean War.

As the U.S. emerged as a super power on the world stage following the end of WWII and with the armistice ending the Korean War, the U.S. sought means to combat communist expansion without having to commit U.S. soldiers in direct action against the Soviets and its allies. Due to the success of the KMAG during the Korean War, military advising and military advisory assistance missions intensified as a means of advancing the ideological role with the formal arrival of the Cold War.[96] Although the origins of the KMAG were rooted in combating communist insurgencies, its missions evolved into greater scope of responsibility, capacity, and capability.[97] The significance of the KMAG's role before and during the Korean War gives credence to the U.S. military advisory mission and the significance of security cooperation and assistance investments to the security of the peninsula.

Unfortunately, in spite of the success of the KMAG, the 500 advisors left behind following the withdrawal of U.S. forces did not pose a significant or credible deterrent for the

---

[95] Finley, *The U.S. Military Experience in Korea*, 9.

[96] Kandall D. Gott and Michael G. Brooks, *Security Assistance: U.S. and International Historical Perspectives* (Fort Leavenworth: Combat Studies Institute Press, 2006), 36.

[97] Ibid.

North Koreans or the Chinese to prevent the invasion. The weak U.S. policy, which set the conditions for the North Korean invasion, eventually lead to a full commitment of U.S. and UN forces in a three year War followed by a permanent U.S. presence on the peninsula until present day. The U.S. government, unable to predict the future impacts of the Cold War in the Pacific, invested in a security strategy focused on the European Theater and placed significantly less resources and political capital into East Asian security issues.

A Shift in Policy: Permanent U.S. Military Presence

Following the Korean War, the U.S. government recognized the importance of the stability and security of the Korean Peninsula for regional stability in East Asia and especially as an ideological platform to deter the spread of communism. The changing strategic, political, and ideological environment of the Cold War drastically shifted U.S. policy to reflect a significant increase in economic and military support for the ROK with emphasis on security and stability on the peninsula. In direct response to the Korean War, American defense expenditure tripled in three years and remained at levels about twice that of 1950 through 1962.[98] The 1953 Mutual Defense Treaty outlined this change in U.S. government foreign policy and brought to fruition a transition from the passive alliance prior to the onset of the war to the position of a staunch ally to the ROK once the realities of communist expansion actualized into an invasion. The spirit of this treaty reflected closer to the "elder brother" relationship King Kojong had aspired for Korea and the U.S. some 50 years earlier. The treaty's narrative of the U.S. commitment to the security of Korea clearly stated:

> "The alliance is primarily intended to protect the integrity of South Korea. It provides deterrence to maintain the armistice on the peninsula and, should deterrence fail, the war-fighting capacity to defeat North Korean aggression. Defeating Pyongyang's aggression does not necessarily mean winning the war to the extent of achieving unification through

---

[98] Donald Kagan, *On the Origins of War* (New York: Doubleday, 1995), 447.

military means. Instead, Washington maintains its security relationship with Seoul for the purpose of preserving peace and stability on the Korean peninsula."[99]

The Mutual Defense Treaty of 1953 laid the framework for the first official U.S. government declaration of a US-ROK alliance framed under the auspices of deterrence and defeating aggression. The strategic end state of preserving peace and stability on the Korean peninsula provided the reason and legitimation for a permanent U.S. military presence in Korea. The United Nations Command (UNC) banner further legitimized stationing U.S. and other UNC forces in Korea and joint defense efforts against potential aggression from North Korea.[100] The deterrence strategy adopted by the U.S.-ROK alliance was two pronged, deterrence by punishment and deterrence by denial.[101] The means and ways in which the alliance executed deterrence by punishment were through the threat of overwhelming U.S. military retaliation through the permanent U.S. presence in South Korea. The means and ways the alliance deterred by denial was through building the capacity of the South Korean military through the increase of security cooperation and assistance programs. The U.S.-ROK alliance combined these two approaches of a strong defense to deny the success of North Korea coupled with the threat of overwhelming retaliation in the event of another invasion from the north.[102]

---

[99] Boose, Hwang, Morgan, Scobell, *Recalibrating the U.S.-Republic of Korea Alliance*, 57-58.

[100] Ibid., 80.

[101] Michael McDevitt, "Deterring North Korean Provocations," *brookings.edu,* February 2011. http://www.brookings.edu/research/papers/2011/02/north-korea-mcdevitt (accessed March 5, 2013), 1.

[102] Ibid.

Permanent U.S. Military Presence in South Korea

In addition to the increased commitment of military advisors to Korea during the Korean War, the most credible and effective means of establishing security and stability on the peninsula was the decision to maintain a permanent forward military presence in Korea following the Korean War. Continuous U.S. combat military presence in Korea for over the last 60 years demonstrates U.S. commitment to security on the Korean peninsula and maintaining regional stability in East Asia. Appendix A quantitatively illustrates the ebb and flow of U.S. military personnel on the peninsula from 1950 to 2008. From the beginning of the Armistice in 1953 to 2008, the average annual U.S. military presence in Korea has been approximately 47,000.[103]

The total percentage of U.S. military personnel committed to Korea in relation to the total number of military personnel following the Armistice in 1953 shows a gradual decline of total U.S. military personnel forward stationed in Korea. Although the percentage of aggregate commitment of personnel deployed to Korea remained relatively stable and unvaried throughout the course of the last 60 year period, the percentage of military personnel committed to Korea since 2003 gradually decreased due to the resource and personnel demands of the wars in Iraq and Afghanistan. According to the Defense Security Cooperation Agency, the most recent personnel statistic for U.S. personnel as of 2008 shows the lowest percentage of personnel dedicated to Korea since the Korean War at 25,061.[104] With the increasing U.S. deficit and growing fiscal constraints on military budgets, U.S. military forward presence in Korea is likely to decline further still.

---

[103] United States Department of Defense, "Active Duty Military Strength & Other Personnel Statistics," http://www.defense.gov/faq/pis/mil_strength.html (accessed December 11, 2012).

[104] Ibid.

Foreign Military Sales and Military Assistance Programs

In conjunction with the commitment of U.S. forces stationed in South Korea, a cornerstone of security assistance efforts to Korea has been the investment in Foreign Military Sales (FMS). The total amount of FMS from fiscal year 1950 to 2011 allowed for building the capacity of the Korean military and equates to an investment of approximately $19.8 Billion, representing 4% of total U.S. FMS sales world wide for that time period (reference Appendix B).[105] The direct benefits of the sale of military equipment to Korea resulted in the modernization of their defensive capabilities, additionally, the substantial technical assistance provided by the U.S. government through licensing agreements with U.S. arms manufacturers lead to the genesis of South Korean arms production and the eventual export of arms in 1977.[106]

Until the early 1970s, South Korea had no arms-producing capability and received on average $250 million annually in U.S. military assistance from 1953 to 1981.[107] Following an unsuccessful North Korean commando raid on the presidential residence in February 1968, the South Korean President announced that South Korea would develop an independent arms production capability and subsequently obtained formal U.S. approval for the development of a defense industry.[108] In addition, the Joint U.S. Military Advisory Group, Korea, provided financial and technical assistance to the South Korean effort to build their independent defense

---

[105] Defense Security Cooperation Agency, "DSCA Historical Facts Book," http://www.dsca.mil/programs/biz-ops/factsbook/Historical%20Facts%20Book%20-%2030%20September%202011.pdf (accessed December 11, 2012).

[106] William Shaw, "South Korean Foreign Military Sales (FMS) Program," (Washington D.C.: Federal Research Division Library of Congress, 1984), iv.

[107] Ibid., 1.

[108] Ibid.

industry.[109] The continued military advisory mission in Korea through this period assisted in building the South Korean capability and capacity to modernize the Korean military, produce their own military arms and munitions, and contributed to the economic growth and stability of the burgeoning country.

Despite the downward trend of U.S. personnel stationed in Korea, the combat capacity and capability of the South Korean military continues to increase and significantly contributes to deterring North Korean aggression. The cumulative effects of U.S. security assistance and cooperation with Korea can be quantified through an examination of the increases in the quantities of ROK's combat equipment. Appendix C illustrates the overall increase of South Korea's military capability as a function of the aggregate number of tanks, artillery, helicopters, combat aircraft, naval destroyers, submarines, and cruisers from 1975 to 2012. As a direct result of the security cooperation and assistance efforts of the U.S. government, South Korea's military capacity increased almost three times in total strength during this 37 year period. As an example, since 1975, the total number of tanks increased from 1,400 to 2,414, combat aircraft from 206 to 390, and submarines from 0 to 23. It is important to note that the increase in the quantity of equipment leveled out over the last 15 years.[110] This is due in large part to the phasing out of legacy equipment and replacing it with modern and technologically advanced war fighting capabilities. The long-term investments in building the capacity of the South Korean military enabled the U.S. government to gradually decrease U.S. military presence on the peninsula and still maintain a credible ROK capability to deter a North Korean invasion.

---

[109] Ibid., 1-2.

[110] The International Institute for Strategic Studies, *The Military Balance 2012,* 2012 ed. (London: Routledge, 2012), "Asia."

Combined U.S. – ROK Military Exercises

The permanent U.S. military presence on the Korean peninsula and the increasing military capacity of the Korean military necessitated combined and joint U.S.-ROK operations in order to validate and exercise the interoperability and effectiveness of their operational capabilities. The strategic underpinning of the bilateral security cooperation agreements between the U.S. and ROK began in April 1968 following an agreement between the U.S. and ROK Presidents to hold annual meetings of defense ministers.[111] The Presidents' intent and goals of this high-level military meeting, officially named the Security Consultative Meeting (SCM), was to enhance bilateral security cooperation. Within the SCM construct, there are five sub committees which report to the SCM, one of which is the Security Cooperation Committee (SCC). The major strategic goals the SCC addresses are the maintenance of ROK-U.S. combined defense system, continuous modernization of the ROK military, dialogue of mid and long-term security cooperation, and concerns about North Korea's missiles and WMD.[112]

With security cooperation as one of the major cornerstone of the SCM's strategic end state and policy guidance, the ways in which the ROK-U.S. execute this policy is through the numerous combined exercises conducted on the peninsula. To name a few, the ROK and U.S. military regularly conduct the Ulchi Freedom Guardian Foal Eagle exercise, the Reception, Staging, Onward Movement and Integration exercise and others. These exercises enable a high level of combined military preparedness and serve as a deterrent to North Korean aggression,

---

[111] Boose, Hwang, Morgan, Scobell, *Recalibrating the U.S.-Republic of Korea Alliance*, 90.

[112] Ibid., 92.

while enhancing the ability of combined militaries to cope with any security crisis on the Korean peninsula.[113]

The security developments between the U.S. and South Korea take place in the context of several concurrent strategic defense approaches. These developments illustrate a shift in posture and strategy leaning more heavily on South Korea capabilities and expanding U.S. military responsibilities to enhance and globalize future defense cooperation.[114] Specifically, in September of 2010, the U.S. government announced the "Strategic Alliance 2015" plan that transfers wartime operational control (OPCON) to the ROK. The South Korean government Defense Reformation Plan 307, which intends to enhance collaboration among the ROK military branches and calls for a new "proactive deterrence" approach calls for a more flexible posture to respond to future attacks, as opposed to the "total war" scenario that has driven much of Seoul's defense planning in the past.[115] This shift towards more ROK responsibility to directly plan and respond to these contingencies is a testament to the security cooperation efforts to build the capacity of the ROK armed forces to achieve the capability to make this transition. The ability to implement this plan is predicated on continued U.S. presence on the peninsula and the continuation of military exercises to ensure the interoperability and coordination between the two militaries.

The shift in U.S. foreign policy following the Korean War drastically altered the commitment to the security of Korea. Since the Armistice in 1953, the approach of the U.S.-ROK alliance has been to present such a formidable posture that North Korea would never believe it

---

[113] Ibid., 98.

[114] Mark E. Manyin, Mary Nikitin, Emma Avery, Ian Rinehart, William H. Cooper, *U.S.-South Korea Relations* (Washington D.C.: Congressional Research Service, 2013), 15.

[115] Manyin, Nikitin, Avery, Rinehart, Cooper, *U.S.-South Korea Relations*, 15.

had an opportunity to forcefully reunify the country under its leadership.[116] The significant

investment in forward stationing military personnel on the peninsula, conducting continuous

combined and joint exercises, in conjunction with the FMS efforts contributed significantly to

building the military and industrial capabilities and capacity of South Korea. The most important

contribution of effective deterrence according to the expected-utility model of deterrence is the

significant increase in the motivation, commitment, and resolve of the U.S. in its alliance with

South Korea.[117] This significant change in policy, driven by the Mutual Defense Treaty of 1953,

precipitated the security cooperation efforts to train and resource the South Korean Army while

maintaining a permanent U.S. presence in South Korea. The strong mutual economic, military,

and political interests developed between the U.S. and South Korea in conjunction with the

significant increase in local military strength since the Korean War set the conditions for a

credible deterrent necessary to dissuade North Korea from a subsequent full scale invasion of

South Korea.

---

[116] Michael McDevitt, "Deterring North Korean Provocations," 1.

[117] Huth and Russett, "What Makes Deterrence Work?" 502.

IMPACT OF NUCLEAR AND BALLISTIC MISSILE THREATS TO SECURITY COOPERATION

The recent advancement of North Korean nuclear and missile capabilities and the threat of proliferation represent one of the United States' biggest foreign policy challenges.[118] One of the main factors which arguably strengthens the U.S.-ROK alliance are the challenges created by North Korea's nuclear and missile programs and the perceptions in Washington and Seoul of whether the Kim regime poses a credible threat of using these capabilities against the alliance.[119] The significant link between North Korean nuclear capability and their developing ballistic missile capability is the attempt to mount a nuclear warhead on North Korea's intermediate-range and long-range missiles.[120] A credible nuclear threat from North Korea will likely keep the nuclear peace, however, it will not prevent – and, indeed, may even facilitate – the use of lower levels of violence.[121] A nuclear capable North Korea will potentially embolden continued conventional acts of hostility, which poses a significant challenge to the effectiveness of security cooperation and assistance efforts for deterring future North Korean aggression.

History of North Korean Nuclear and Ballistic Missile Development

The U.S. began tracking the progress of the North Korean nuclear program in the early 1980s and discovered by 1986 that North Korea was capable of producing 6 kilograms of

---

[118] Mark E. Manyin, *Kim Jong-Il's Death: Implications for North Korea's Stability and U.S. Policy* (Washington D.C.: Congressional Research Service, 2012), 1.

[119] Manyin, Nikitin, Avery, Rinehart, Cooper, *U.S.-South Korea Relations*, 5.

[120] Mary Nikitin, *North Korea's Nuclear Weapons: Technical Issues* (Washington D.C.: Congressional Research Service, 2013), Summary.

[121] Robert J. Art and Kenneth N. Waltz, *The Use of Force: Military Power and International Politics* (Oxford: Rowman & Littlefield Publishers, Inc., 2004), 95.

plutonium a year with the material and technical support from the Soviet Union.[122] In 1994,

through U.S. diplomatic efforts, North Korea froze its plutonium programs and eventually

dismantled them in return for several kinds of assistance.[123]After an eight-year freeze, North

Korea broke this agreement and restarted its reactor and reprocessing plant in 2002.[124] The

persistence of North Korea's nuclear weapons program led to a U.S. national strategy to combat

weapons of mass destruction. This U.S. policy reserved the right to respond with overwhelming

force, including conventional and nuclear capabilities, to the use of weapons of mass destruction

(WMD) against the United States, its overseas forces, or its allies.[125] Despite the efforts of this

policy and international pressure by the members of the Six-Party Talks – The U.S., South Korea,

Japan, China, Russia, and North Korea – North Korea continued its nuclear program and

eventually tested a nuclear devise in October 2006.[126] Six Party Talks have not been held since

2009 and subsequently North Korea conducted its second nuclear test in 2009.[127]

Most recently, North Korea demonstrated technological advancements in both their

nuclear and ballistic missile capabilities. For the first time on December 12, 2012, North Korea

successfully launched a three-stage Unha-3 rocket demonstrating their long-range missile

capability to potentially put U.S. territory into target range.[128] In direct response to this

---

[122] Nikitin, *North Korea's Nuclear Weapons: Technical Issues*, 1.

[123] Ibid.

[124] Ibid.

[125] Boose, Hwang, Morgan, Scobell, *Recalibrating the U.S.-Republic of Korea*, 6.

[126] Nikitin, 1.

[127] Ibid., 2.

[128] Patrick M. Cronin, "Rescind North Korea's License to Provoke," *CNN.com,* January 29, 2013. http://www.cnn.com/2013/01/29/opinion/cronin-north-korea-strategy/index.html?iid=article_sidebar (accessed January 30, 2013).

provocation and violation of existing United Nations Security Council resolutions and missile

moratorium, the United Nations Security Council unanimously passed Resolution 2087, which

strengthened existing sanctions, curbed the travel and potentially the finances of the agencies and

senior officials responsible for the rocket launch.[129] The heightened tensions created by the

successful launch of the Unha-3 rocket were further exacerbated by a third nuclear test conducted

on February 12, 2013, further complicating diplomatic efforts towards denuclearization.[130]

Strategic Context of a Nuclear North Korean

Much like the foreign politics of the "Hermit Kingdom" leading up to King Kojong's

attempts at social, political, and military reform in Korea, North Korea continues to espouse an

isolationist foreign policy. North Korea demonstrates a lack of any serious commitment to

reform, to engagement, and to opening up to the world, which is why the North perpetually

neglects opportunities to negotiate and why they did not respond effectively to the opportunity

raised by the 9/11 incidents to deepen engagement with the United States.[131] Instead of diplomacy

through engagement and reform, North Korea leverages the practice of brinksmanship to achieve

international objectives such as extracting aid and other benefits from the outside world.[132] The

primary source of national power for North Korea is its military power and maintaining a

weapons of mass destruction (WMD) program, which has become integral to the regime's

---

[129] Cronin, "Rescind North Korea's License to Provoke," *CNN.com,* January 29, 2013. http://www.cnn.com/2013/01/29/opinion/cronin-north-korea-strategy/index.html?iid=article_sidebar (accessed January 30, 2013).

[130] Nikitin, *North Korea's Nuclear Weapons: Technical Issues,* 2.

[131] Boose, Hwang, Morgan, Scobell, *Recalibrating the U.S.-Republic of Korea,* vi.

[132] Mark E. Manyin, *Kim Jong-Il's Death: Implications for North Korea's Stability and U.S. Policy* (Washington D.C.: Congressional Research Service, 2012), 7.

survival.[133] North Korea maintains the fourth-largest standing armed forces, however, the state of their equipment, training, morale, and operational readiness is believed to be poor.[134]

Although the conventional military balance on the peninsula may indeed favor the South Korea and the United States, North Korea's nuclear capabilities and its previous stockpile of chemical arms complementing its conventional capabilities poses a significant military threat to South Korea and the Pacific region.[135] According to the U.S. Congressional Research Service, U.S. defense analysts have begun to coalesce around the consensus that North Korea is committed to maintaining a minimum number of nuclear weapons as a security guarantor from a pre-emptive strike by the U.S. or South Korea.[136] Because South Korea does not possess nuclear weapon capabilities, it is included under the U.S. "nuclear umbrella," known as the extended deterrence policy. Extended deterrence is defined as "the ability of U.S. military forces, particularly nuclear forces, to deter attack on U.S. allies and thereby reassure them."[137] This U.S. nuclear deterrence policy remains important for South Korea to dissuade North Korea from launching a nuclear as well as a conventional attack.[138]

---

[133] Manyin, *Kim Jong-Il's Death*, 7.

[134] *The Military Balance 2012,* 2012 ed. (London: Routledge, 2012), s.vv. "Asia."

[135] Michael E. O'Hanlon, *The Wounded Giant: America's Armed Forces in an Age of Austerity* (New York: The Penguin Press, 2011), chap. 1, under "Introduction," Kindle eBook, Loc 163.

[136] Emma Chanlett-Avery, Ian E. Rinehart, *North Korea: U.S. Relations, Nuclear Diplomacy, and Internal Situation* (Washington D.C.: Congressional Research Service, 2013), 5.

[137] Richard C. Bush, Vanda Felbab-Brown, Martin S. Indyk, Michael O'Hanlon, Steven Pifer, Kenneth M. Pollack, *U.S. Nuclear and Extended Deterrence: Considerations and Challenges* (Washington D.C.: Brookings Institution, 2010), 1.

[138] Ibid., 36.

Strategic Context of Ballistic Missile Defense in South Korea

The demonstrated advances of North Korean ballistic missile capabilities by the successful launch of the Uhna-3 coupled with the potential of their ability to weaponize their nuclear capability onto the missiles further complicates a deterrent and defensive challenge for the U.S. and South Korea. North Korean ballistic missiles are an instrument of coercion and give them legitimacy through the threat of the use of this hard power in order to maintain heightened political and military tensions. North Korea continues to pursue the advancement and production of ballistic missiles because they can be used effectively against the formidable air power of the U.S and South Korean Air Forces without the expense of maintaining and training a modern Air Force. Ballistic missiles provide North Korea with a high volume of preemptive strike capabilities at a relatively minimal cost. The burgeoning possibility of a North Korean ballistic missile with a nuclear payload precipitates a requirement for not only deterrence against the use of this capability, but also an effective defense. Maintaining U.S. missile defense forces in South Korea coupled with the security assistance and cooperation efforts through FMS programs to field South Korea with BMD capabilities is a cornerstone to deterring North Korean ballistic missile and nuclear threats.

The direct purpose of U.S. Ballistic Missile Defense (BMD) forces in South Korea is to defeat a North Korean ballistic missile attack in order to deny gains by frustrating a potential attack.[139] The effect of BMD increases the freedom of action of the U.S. and South Korea by permitting less destructive or less immediate retaliation, decreasing the risk to carry out preemptive attacks, and would reduce the risks and potential costs of a conventional war with North Korea. This increased freedom of action created by a credible BMD capability translates

---

[139] Bush, Felbab-Brown, Indyk, O'Hanlon, Pifer, Pollack, *U.S. Nuclear and Extended Deterrence: Considerations and Challenges*, 16.

into less promising options for North Korea and contributes to the overall deterrence of both a nuclear and conventional attack from the North.[140]

In June 2012, U.S. Secretary of Defense Leon Panetta emphasized new initiatives on missile defense and reiterated the U.S. commitment to maintain current troop levels in South Korea.[141] In addition to continued U.S. BMD support to Korea, South Korea's defense ministry has said that it will prioritize its own defense systems against North Korea's missile and nuclear threats, including Aegis combat destroyers, missile interceptors, and early warning radars.[142] The continuous increase in U.S. and South Korean investment in missile defense capabilities are due to its increasing contributions to deterrence, both for protection of the American homeland and of U.S. allies and partners.[143]

The advancement of North Korea's nuclear weapon capabilities destabilizes the Pacific region and creates significant foreign policy challenges for the U.S. and its allies in the region. The unpredictability of the North Korean regime and the uncertainty of the probability of a preemptive nuclear attack challenge the effectiveness of U.S. security cooperation and assistance efforts to South Korea as a deterrent. North Korea will continue to leverage their nuclear weapon capability to reinforce their rhetoric of their intention to destroy the U.S. and South Korea in order to benefit from the fear and tension it causes in the region.[144] Because South Korea does not

---

[140] Robert J. Art and Kenneth N. Waltz, *The Use of Force: Military Power and International Politics* (Oxford: Rowman & Littlefield Publishers, Inc., 2004), 341.

[141] Mark E. Manyin, Mary Nikitin, Emma Avery, Ian Rinehart, William H. Cooper, *U.S.-South Korea Relations* (Washington D.C.: Congressional Research Service, 2013), 13.

[142] Ibid.

[143] Bush, Felbab-Brown, Indyk, O'Hanlon, Pifer, Pollack, *U.S. Nuclear and Extended Deterrence: Considerations and Challenges*, 16.

[144] Henry D. Sokoloski, *Next Arms Race* (Carlisle: Strategic Studies Institute, 2012), 408.

have a nuclear weapon capability, the U.S. policy of extended deterrence provides a credible nuclear deterrence against North Korea; however, the necessity of a credible, technologically advanced conventional force can also substitute the deterrent capabilities provided by nuclear weapons.[145] Despite the lack of a South Korean nuclear weapons program, the security cooperation and assistance efforts over the course of the last 60 years demonstrates the importance of building the conventional capacity of the South Korean military. Huth and Russett's expected-utility model of deterrence hypothesizes that strategic nuclear superiority is unlikely to be the most effective means for providing security, but the combination of local military strength and the ties of mutual interest.[146] If this theory is true, the efficacy of the South Korean conventional forces and the ties of mutual interest between the U.S. and the ROK are the two most important factors to effectively deter both a conventional and nuclear North Korean attack.

---

[145] Sokoloski, *Next Arms Race*, 387.

[146] Huth and Russett, "What Makes Deterrence Work?" 524.

CONCLUSION

The tumultuous history of U.S. security cooperation and assistance to the Republic of Korea eventually led to one of the strongest diplomatic, military, and economic alliances in the Pacific. The ineffectiveness of security cooperation and assistance in the early U.S.-ROK history was due in large part to the U.S. policy of positive neutrality. This policy drastically changed fifty years following General Dye's initial attempts to export U.S. foreign policy. Following the end of WWII, the U.S., as a burgeoning world power, began investing politically, economically, and militarily in the security of Korea. The KMAG was the first security cooperation effort that resulted in significantly increasing the capacity of the South Korean security forces and laid the foundation for future U.S.-ROK military engagements and capacity building.

The shift in U.S. foreign policy following the Korean War drastically altered the commitment to the security of Korea and established an enduring commitment of U.S. forces on the peninsula. Since the Armistice in 1953, the change in the strategic and geopolitical importance of the ROK precipitated a further increase in security cooperation and assistance activities. The significant investment in forward stationing military personnel on the peninsula, conducting continuous combined and joint exercises, in conjunction with the FMS efforts contributed significantly to building the military and industrial capabilities and capacity of South Korea. The change in U.S. policy and the resulting increase in commitment and investment in the security of South Korea set the conditions for a capable and credible deterrent to dissuade North Korea from a subsequent full-scale invasion of South Korea. The strength and resolve of the U.S. commitment to the security cooperation and assistance to South Korea echoes in the 2012 Defense Strategic Guidance, which states:

> "While the U.S. military will continue to contribute to security globally, *we will of necessity rebalance toward the Asia-Pacific region.* Our relationships with Asian allies and key partners are critical to the future stability and growth of the region…Furthermore, we will maintain peace on the Korean Peninsula by effectively

working with allies and other regional states to deter and defend against provocation from North Korea, which is actively pursuing a nuclear weapons program." [147]

In spite of the complex challenges a North Korean nuclear threat poses in South Korea, the U.S. security assistance and cooperation efforts and U.S. military presence on the peninsula continues to create a credible deterrence from a North Korean conventional and nuclear threat. In an increasingly globalized world, the world in general will continue to benefit from the current international order in which America is the strongest power and helps lead a broader alliance system involving most of the world's other major powers. [148] Peace in East Asia and the Pacific is a reflection of the foreign policy successes following the Korean War and because of it, the world's wealth and strength is found among alliances and security assistance efforts with countries such as Korea. [149] Continued domestic, international, and economic constraints make the idea of reduced security commitments appealing. The truth that South Korea's military is better than before, while North Korea's is less strong overall should not preclude us from ignoring the North Korean threat. [150] North Korea's WMD threat and its expanding ballistic missile program coupled with its volatile domestic political landscape makes U.S. continued security assistance and cooperation critical for the stability of the region. U.S. continuous presence coupled with building the ROK army's capacity continues to keep North Korea at bay.

As illustrated during the periods of 1882-1905 and 1945-1950, the lack of U.S. interest in security of the ROK in conjunction with minimal local military strength led to the ROK's

---

[147] U.S. Department of Defense, "Sustaining U.S. Global Leadership: Priorities for 21st Century Defense" (Washington: U.S. Department of Defense, 2012), 2.

[148] O'Hanlon, *The Wounded Giant: America's Armed Forces in an Age of Austerity*, chap. 1, under "Introduction," Kindle eBook, Loc 134.

[149] Ibid, Loc 2267.

[150] Ibid, Loc 163.

inability to maintain their sovereignty and deter aggression. The significant investment in security cooperation activities in the ROK following the Korean War enabled the U.S. to gradually withdraw forces from the peninsula while simultaneously building the ROKA capacity to deter a North Korean invasion. Since 2008, the magic number of U.S. military presence on the peninsula to achieve deterrence in Korea declined to around 25,000.[151] Without question, the security cooperation and assistance efforts of the U.S. significantly increased the ROK military strength and enabled the U.S. to justify the relatively low number of U.S. military presence. The increase in local ROK military strength and continued U.S. interest in the security and economy of South Korea provide the greatest probability of deterring a North Korean attack according to Ruth and Hussett's theory of deterrence. However, Ruth and Hussett's theory on deterrence suggests that the most important contribution to effective deterrence is maintaining and strengthening the ties of mutual interest among nation-states in an open global economic system.[152] Future research and studies should be conducted to ascertain the most efficient and effective balance of local military strength, both U.S. and ROK forces, assuming strong ties of mutual interest between the U.S. and South Korea continue through the foreseeable future.

---

[151] United States Department of Defense, "Active Duty Military Strength & Other Personnel Statistics," http://www.defense.gov/faq/pis/mil_strength.html (accessed December 11, 2012).

[152] Huth and Russett, "What Makes Deterrence Work?" 524.

APPENDIX A: MILITARY PERSONNEL STRENGTH IN KOREA

Table 1. Military personnel strength in Korea from 1950-2008

| Compiled from the Military Personnel Strength Figures on the U.S. Department of Defense Website (www.defense.gov) | | | | |
Year	Military Personnel in Korea	Military Personnel OCONUS	Total Military Personnel	% of Personnel in Korea/OCONUS	% of Personnel in Korea/Total
1950	510	328,392	1,460,261	0.16%	0.03%
1953	326,863	1,216,688	3,555,067	26.86%	9.19%
1954	225,590	1,120,175	3,279,579	20.14%	6.88%
1955	75,328	927,851	2,930,863	8.12%	2.57%
1956	68,810	881,548	2,795,460	7.81%	2.46%
1957	71,043	927,537	2,758,069	7.66%	2.58%
1958	46,024	811,254	2,598,015	5.67%	1.77%
1959	49,827	708,618	2,492,449	7.03%	2.00%
1960	55,864	685,582	2,492,037	8.15%	2.24%
1961	57,694	705,109	2,552,912	8.18%	2.26%
1962	60,947	766,628	2,687,690	7.95%	2.27%
1963	56,910	731,045	2,695,240	7.78%	2.11%
1964	62,596	737,433	2,690,141	8.49%	2.33%
1965	58,636	832,364	2,723,800	7.04%	2.15%
1966	47,076	1,051,893	3,229,209	4.48%	1.46%
1967	55,057	1,228,538	3,411,931	4.48%	1.61%
1968	62,263	1,074,983	3,175,263	5.79%	1.96%
1969	66,531	1,041,094	3,132,766	6.39%	2.12%
1970	52,197	875,423	2,718,027	5.96%	1.92%
1971	40,740	682,672	2,392,412	5.97%	1.70%
1972	41,600	496,830	2,111,403	8.37%	1.97%
1973	41,864	456,242	2,006,926	9.18%	2.09%
1974	40,387	420,684	1,945,818	9.60%	2.08%
1975	40,204	407,287	1,901,661	9.87%	2.11%
1976	39,133	389,894	1,866,960	10.04%	2.10%
1977	40,075	459,385	2,074,543	8.72%	1.93%
1978	41,565	471,874	2,062,404	8.81%	2.02%
1979	39,018	458,424	2,027,494	8.51%	1.92%
1980	38,780	488,726	2,050,826	7.93%	1.89%
1981	38,254	501,832	2,082,897	7.62%	1.84%
1982	39,194	528,484	2,108,612	7.42%	1.86%
1983	38,705	519,517	2,123,349	7.45%	1.82%
1984	40,785	510,730	2,138,157	7.99%	1.91%
1985	41,718	515,367	2,151,032	8.09%	1.94%
1986	43,133	525,328	2,169,112	8.21%	1.99%
1987	44,674	523,702	2,174,217	8.53%	2.05%
1988	45,501	540,588	2,138,213	8.42%	2.13%
1989	44,461	509,873	2,130,229	8.72%	2.09%
1990	41,344	609,422	2,046,144	6.78%	2.02%
1991	40,062	447,572	1,986,259	8.95%	2.02%
1992	35,743	344,065	1,807,177	10.39%	1.98%
1993	34,830	308,020	1,705,103	11.31%	2.04%
1994	36,796	286,594	1,610,490	12.84%	2.28%
1995	36,016	238,064	1,518,224	15.13%	2.37%
1996	36,539	240,421	1,471,722	15.20%	2.48%
1997	35,663	227,258	1,438,562	15.69%	2.48%
1998	36,890	259,871	1,406,830	14.20%	2.62%
1999	35,913	252,763	1,385,703	14.21%	2.59%
2000	36,565	257,817	1,384,338	14.18%	2.64%
2001	37,605	254,788	1,385,116	14.76%	2.71%
2002	37,743	230,484	1,411,634	16.38%	2.67%
2003	41,145	252,764	1,434,377	16.28%	2.87%
2004	40,840	287,802	1,426,836	14.19%	2.86%
2005	30,983	290,997	1,389,394	10.65%	2.23%
2006	29,086	284,967	1,384,968	10.21%	2.10%
2007	27,014	295,003	1,379,551	9.16%	1.96%
2008	25,061	288,550	1,401,757	8.69%	1.79%

Source: United States Department of Defense[153]

---

[153] United States Department of Defense, "Active Duty Military Strength & Other Personnel Statistics," http://www.defense.gov/faq/pis/mil_strength.html (accessed December 11, 2012).

APPENDIX B: FOREIGN MILITARY SALES STATISTICS

Table 2. Foreign military sales in Korea from 1950-2011

	FY 1950 to FY 2003	FY 2004	FY 2005	FY 2006	FY 2007	FY 2008	FY 2009	FY 2010	FY 2011	FY 1950 to FY 2011
Korea	14,626,323	337,012	401,647	408,018	816,216	1,080,972	714,486	967,576	453,015	19,805,266
East Asia & Pacific	68,412,248	2,241,982	1,840,632	4,179,185	4,196,606	4,264,706	5,659,822	3,646,951	7,816,669	102,258,801
Worldwide	345,365,184	13,586,545	8,818,134	17,521,803	17,697,654	28,234,599	29,629,492	22,560,882	26,404,176	509,918,469
% Korea/EA & Pacific	21%	15%	22%	10%	19%	25%	13%	27%	6%	19%
% Korea/Worldwide	4%	2%	5%	2%	5%	4%	2%	4%	2%	4%

Source: Defense Security Cooperation Agency[154]

---

[154] Defense Security Cooperation Agency, "DSCA Historical Facts Book," http://www.dsca.mil/programs/biz-ops/factsbook/Historical%20Facts%20Book%20-%2030%20September%202011.pdf (accessed December 11, 2012).

APPENDIX C: SOUTH KOREAN MILITARY EQUIPMENT FROM 1975 TO 2012

Table 3. ROK military equipment capacity from 1975-2012

	1975	1980	1985	1990	1995	2000	2005	2012
Tanks	1400	1430	1200	1550	2050	2330	2330	2414
Artillery	2000	2000	3000	4000	4500	4540	4589	4853
Fighter Aircraft	206	330	325	380	461	555	540	390
Helicopters	15	61	250	365	538	404	424	457
Destroyers	7	10	11	9	7	6	6	6
Submarines	0	0	0	3	6	19	20	23
Cruisers	0	0	0	0	0	0	0	2

Source: The Military Balance 2012[155]

Table 4. Bar chart of ROK military equipment capacity from 1975-2012

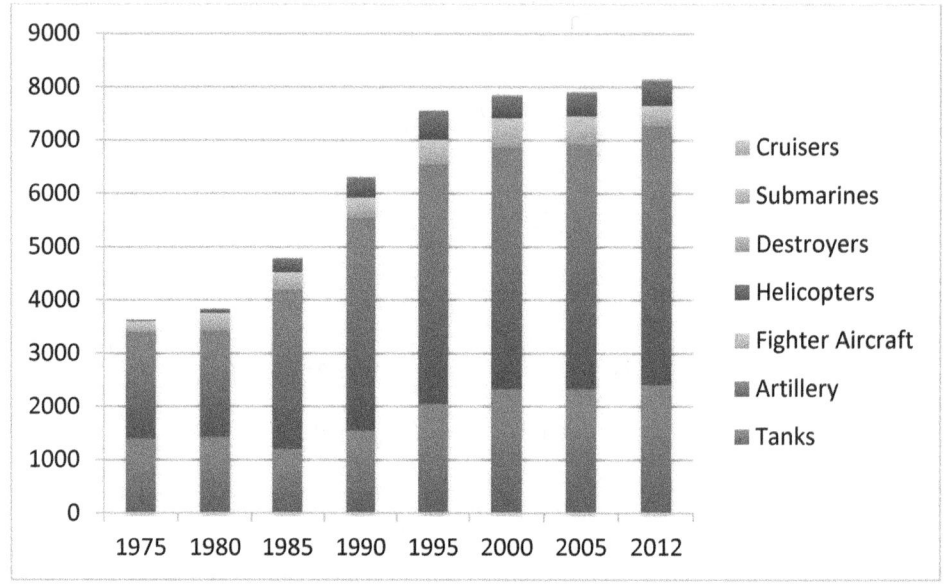

Source: The Military Balance 2012[156]

[155] The International Institute for Strategic Studies, *The Military Balance 2012,* 2012 ed. (London: Routledge, 2012), "Asia."

[156] Ibid.

BIBLIOGRAPHY

Alexander, Bevin. *Korea: The First War We Lost.* NY: Hippocrene, 1986.

Appleman, Roy E. *Ridgway Duels for Korea.* College Station, TX: TX A&M, 1990.

Art, Robert J., and Kenneth N. Waltz. *The Use of Force: Military Power and International Politics.* Sixth. Oxford: Rowman & Littlefield Publishers, Inc., 2004.

Bishop, Donald M. "Shared Failure: American Military Advisors in Korea, 1888-1896." *Transitions of the Royal Asiatic Society, Korea Branch 58.* 1983.

Boose, Donald W., Balbina Y. Hwang, Patrick Morgan, and Andrew Scobell. *Recalibrating the U.S.-Republic of Korea Alliance.* Special Report, Carlisle: Strategic Studies Institute, 2003.

Bush, Richard C., Vanda Felbab-Brown, Martin S. Indyk, Michael O'Hanlon, Steven Pifer, and Kenneth M. Pollack. "U.S. Nuclear and Extended Deterrence: Considerations and Challenges." Washington D.C.: Brookings Institution, May 2010.

Central Intelligence Agency. *Implementation of Soviet Objectives in Korea.* Harry S. Truman Library, 1947.

Central Intelligence Group. *The Situation in Korea.* Harry S. Truman Library, 1947.

Chanlett-Avery, Emma, and Ian E. Rinehart. "North Korea: U.S. Relations, Nuclear Diplomacy, and Internal Situation." Washington D.C.: Congressional Research Service, January 4, 2013.

Clausewitz, Carl Von. *On War.* Princeton: Princeton University Press, 1976.

Collins, Lawton J. *War in Peacetime: The History and Lessons of Korea.* Boston: Houghton Mifflin, 1969.

Condit, Kenneth W. *History of the Joint Chiefs of Staff: The Joint Chiefs of Staff and National Policy Volume II 1947-1949.* Washington, DC: Office of Joint History, 1996.

Cronin, Patrick M. "Rescind North Korea's License to Provoke." *CNN.com,* January 29, 2013.

Cumings, Bruce. *The Korean War: A History.* NY: Modern Library, 2010.

Defense Security Cooperation Agency. *DSCA Historical Facts Book.* http://www.dsca.mil/programs/biz-ops/factsbook/Historical%20Facts%20Book%20-%2030%20September%202011.pdf (accessed December 11, 2012).

Department of Defense. *Active Duty Military Strength & Other Personnel Statistics.* http://www.defense.gov/faq/pis/mil_strength.html (accessed December 11, 2012).

Department of Defense. Joint Publication (JP) 3-0. *Joint Operations*. Washington D.C.: Government Printing Office, 11 August 2011.

Department of Defense. "Sustaining U.S. Global Leadership: Priorities for 21st Century Defense." Washington, January 2012.

Dupuy, R. Ernest, and Trevor Dupuy. *The Encyclopedia of Military History from 3500 B.C. to the Present*. New York: Harper & Row, 1986.

Ecker, Richard E. *Korean Battle Chronology: Unit-by-Unit United States Casualty Figures and Medal of Honor Citations*. Jefferson, NC: McFarland & Co., Inc., 2005.

Edwards, Paul M. *Combat Operations of the Korean War: Ground, Air, Sea, Special and Covert*. Jefferson, NC: McFarland, 2010.

—. *The Inchon Landing, Korea, 1950: An Annotated Bibliography*. Westport: Greenwood Press, 1994.

Fehrenbach. *This Kind of War: The Classic Korean War History*. New York: Brassey's, 1963.

Finley, James P. *The US Military Experience in Korea, 1871-1982: In the Vanguard of ROK-US Relations*. San Francisco: Command Historian's Office, Secretary Joint Staff, Hqs, USFK/EUSA, 1983.

Forty, George. *At War in Korea*. London: Allan, 1982.

Freedman, Lawrence. *Transformation of Strategic Affairs*. New York: Routledge for the International Institute for Strategic Studies, 2006.

Gaddis, John Lewis, and Paul Nitze. "NSC 68 and the Soviet Threat Reconsidered." *International Security* 4, no. 4 (1980).

Gott, Kendall D., and Michael G. Brooks. *Security Assistance: U.S. and International Historical Perspectives*. Fort Leavenworth: Combat Studies Institute Press, 2006.

Hastings, Max. *The Korean War*. NY: Simon & Schuster, 1987.

Hausrath, Alfred H. *The KMAG Advisor: Role and Problems of the Military Advisor in Developing an Indigenous Army for Combat Operations in Korea*. Chevy Chase: The Johns Hopkins University Operations Research Office, 1957.

Hickey, Michael. *The Korean War: The West Confronts Communism*. Woodstock, NY: The Overlook Press, 1999.

Huth, Paul, and Bruce Russet. "What Makes Deterrence Work? Cases from 1900 to 1980." *World Politics* 36, no. 4 (July 1984): 496-526.

Kagan, Donald. *On the Origins of War*. New York: Doubleday, 1995.

Lee, Yur-Bok, and Wayne Patterson. *Korean-American Relations.* Albany: State University of New York Press, 1999.

Lord, Carnes. "Crisis Management: A Primer." *IASPS Research Papers in Strategy.* no. No. 7. Institute for Advanced Strategic and Political Studies, August 1998.

MacArthur, Douglas. *Summary of Messages Exchanged Between CINCFE and the JCS Concerning the Inchon Landing Conducted in Korea in September 1950.* Washington, D.C.: Department of the Army, 1954.

Manyin, Mark E. *Kim Jong-Il's Death: Implications for North Korea's Stability and U.S. Policy.* Washington D.C.: Congressional Research Service, 2012.

Manyin, Mark, Mary Nikitin, Emma Avery, Ian Rinehart, and William Cooper. *U.S.-South Korea Relations.* Washington D.C.: Congressional Research Service, 2013.

Marshall, S.L.A. *The Military History of the Korean War.* NY: Watts, 1963.

McDevitt, Michael. "Deterring North Korean Provocations." *www.brookings.edu.* February 2011. http://www.brookings.edu/research/papers/2011/02/north-korea-mcdevitt (accessed March 5, 2013).

Memorandum for the President. *Clearance of Proposed Legislation for Aid to Korea.* Harry S. Truman Library, 1947.

Memorandum for the President. *Training of Korean Coast Guard by United States Coast Guard Personnel.* Harry S. Truman Library, 1946.

Millett, Allan Reed. *The War for Korea, 1950-1951: They Came from the North.* Lawrence: University Press of Kansas, 2010.

National Security Council. *A Report to the President: The Position of the United States with Respect to Korea.* Harry S. Truman Library, 1948.

Odierno, Ray. "The Force of Tomorrow." *ForeignPolicy.com*, February 4, 2013.

O'Hanlon, Michael E. *The Science of War.* Princeton, NJ: Princeton University Press, 2009.

—. *The Wounded Giant: America's Armed Forces in an Age of Austerity.* New York: The Penguin Press, 2011.

Sanger, David E. *South Koreans and U.S. to Stage a Joint Exericse.* New York: The New York Times, November 23, 2010.

Shaw, William. *South Korean Foreign Military Sales (FMS) Program.* Washington D.C.: Federal Research Division Library of Congress, 1984.

Smith, Steve. "The Increasing Insecurity of Security Studies: Conceptualizing Security in the Last Twenty Years." *Contemporary Security Policy*, 1999: 72-101.

Sokolski, Henry D. "Next Arms Race." Carlisle: Strategic Studies Institute, July 2012.

The International Institute for Strategic Studies. *The Military Balance 2012*. London: Routledge, 2012.

Thomas, Robert C. *The War in Korea, 1950-53: A Military Study of the War in Korea Up to the Signing of the Cease Fire*. Aldershot: Gale, 1954.

Truman, Harry. *Draft Message on Korea*. Harry S. Truman Library, 1947.

Weinert, Richard P. "The Original KMAG." *Military Review* XLV, no. 6 (June 1965): 93-99.

Williamson, Murray, and MacGregor Knox. *The Dynamics of Military Revolution: 1300-2050*. New York: Cambridge University Press, 2001.